Maddy's Manners

Kenyae L. Reese, PhD

www.TrueVinePublishing.org

Maddy's Manners
Kenyae L. Reese, PhD
Illustration by FX and Color Studio

Published by
True Vine Publishing Co.
810 Dominican Dr.
Nashville, TN 37228
www.TrueVinePublishing.org

Copyright © 2023 by Kenyae L. Reese, PhD

All rights reserved. No part of this book may be reproduced in any form including by any electronic or mechanical means, (including information storage and retrieval or mechanical means) without permission in writing from the publisher, except by a reviewer who may quote brief passages in a review.

ISBN: 978-1-956469-84-4
ISBN: 978-1-956469-85-1

Printed in the United States of America—First Printing

Editor La Tanya Rogers, PhD

Song: Etiquette is Fantastic
Songwriter: Kenyae L. Reese, PhD
Producer: Christopher Blackmon

Vocalists:
Kenyae L. Reese, PhD
Gael Alcala
Valentina Alcala
Irie Burum
Braeden Carlton
Rosa Underwood
Donna Blackmon

Special Thanks to Tony Sinkfield for designing the B & D hand illustration

Dedication

To my readers of all ages, just remember that you were made for greatness.

Acknowledgments

I am truly grateful to my parents, Otha and John Reese, whose work ethic, philanthropy efforts, and etiquette training over the course of my childhood sparked a passion in me for etiquette that has never ceased. Mom, I used to tease you for having a "museum of a house" that was featured in magazines no less; but, oh, how I appreciate that upbringing even more now! Thank you!

Words can't express my gratitude to my sister, Dr. La Tanya Rogers. After all, she is the best writer and thinker that I know. There's not much in this world she can't do. She leads by example! I'm eternally grateful for her gifts, talents, and willingness to share them with me. I love you! Bese Saka!

To my dear Olivia and Dexter, my niece and nephew, who were great sounding boards during this process. Aunt Keke is forever proud of you. You two were indeed made for greatness! Always remember the three most important words that I taught you. No, it's not I love you, although that's true. The other three words—you know what they are, lol!

I'm forever grateful to my extended family—the entire Miller, Reese, Woods, and Wiseman families for the great generational legacy bestowed upon our family. I would especially like to recognize my Uncle Harry Dan Reese, my Aunt Leola Davis, my cousin La Tosha Wiseman, and my 108-year-old grandmother Mrs. Elizabeth Woods Wiseman (Walter, deceased) for always providing a listening ear.

Thank you to my Hampton University, University of Georgia, Clemson, and Harvard families. I would also like to thank my Hillsboro Burros and Head Magnet families, and countless other friends and colleagues.

To my dearest friend Shaun Gholston (best copy editor ever), Victor Chatman who gave me the nudge to publish, Dr. Kawonia Mull, Dr. Markethia Mull, Kiera Easley, Renee Bobb, and Donte Cleaves who re-introduced me to Timothy Bond of True Vine Publishing. Tim, thanks for patience and believing in Maddy. We're going places!

Maddy would not be complete without the sing-along song "Etiquette is Fantastic". The song has been on my heart and mind for more than ten years. Thanks to Christopher Blackmon, music producer, his wife Donna Blackmon, and the Chords and Voices choir for putting my words to music. Thanks to Christopher, the "Etiquette is Fantastic" song is living and breathing and was masterfully made.

Finally, thank you to my readers who will keep Maddy alive for generations to come. Please gift her to the children (and adults) who need her most.

I'm overcome with joy! Soli Deo Gloria!

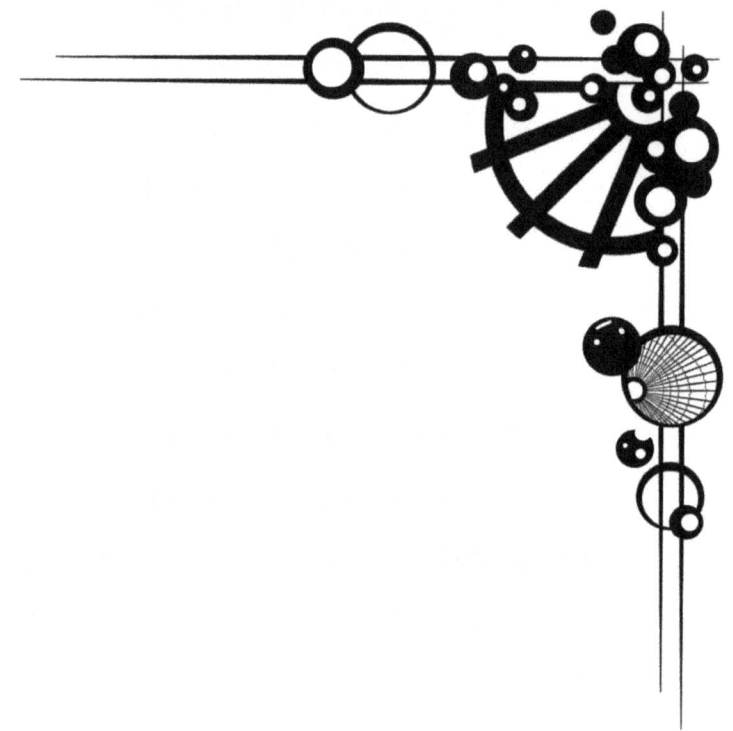

Tonight is the night. I cannot wait.
My first dinner party, and there's so much at stake.

The guests include friends and parents, too.
My favorite Bear Bear will make a debut.

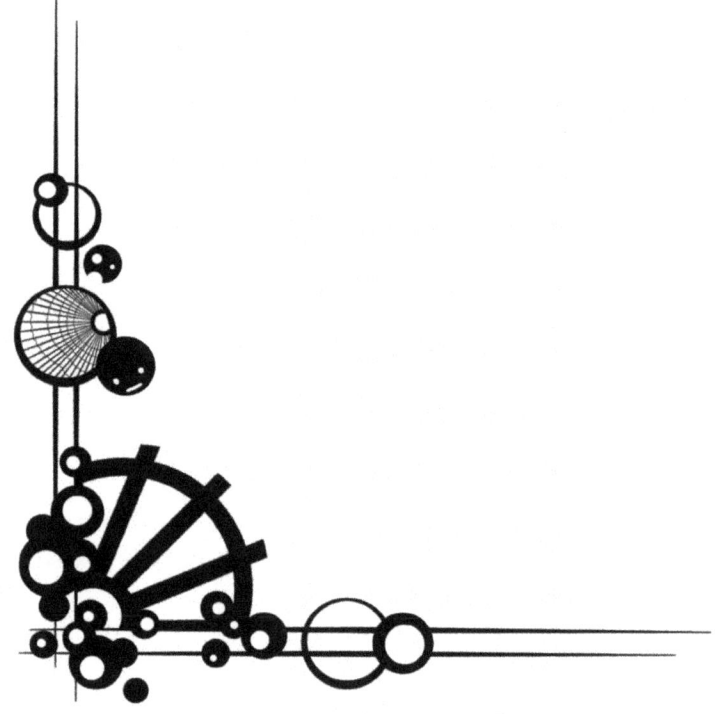

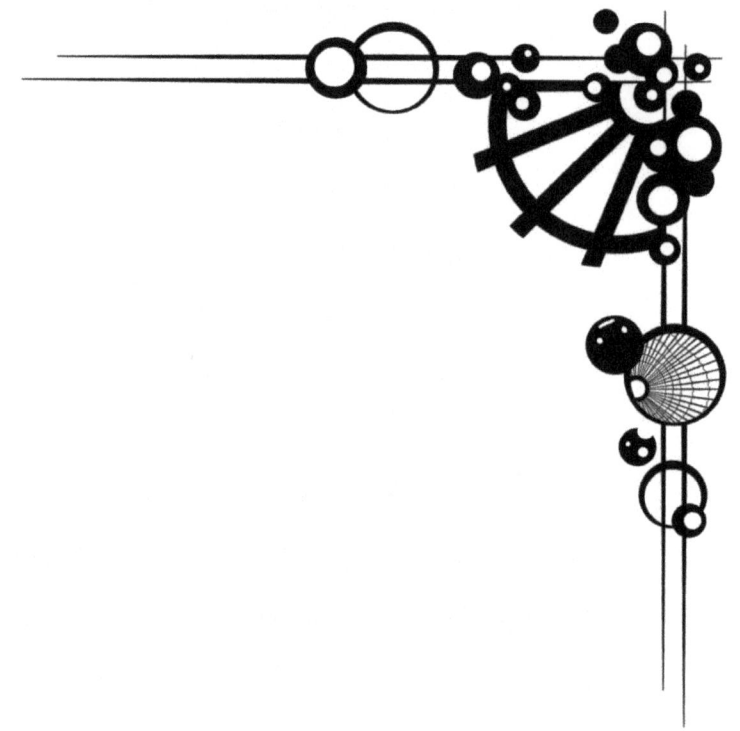

My mom plans to show me all I need to do
to be a good hostess and keep my manners, too.

She writes out a list. It's a check list of facts.
I glance at the clock to help me stay on track.

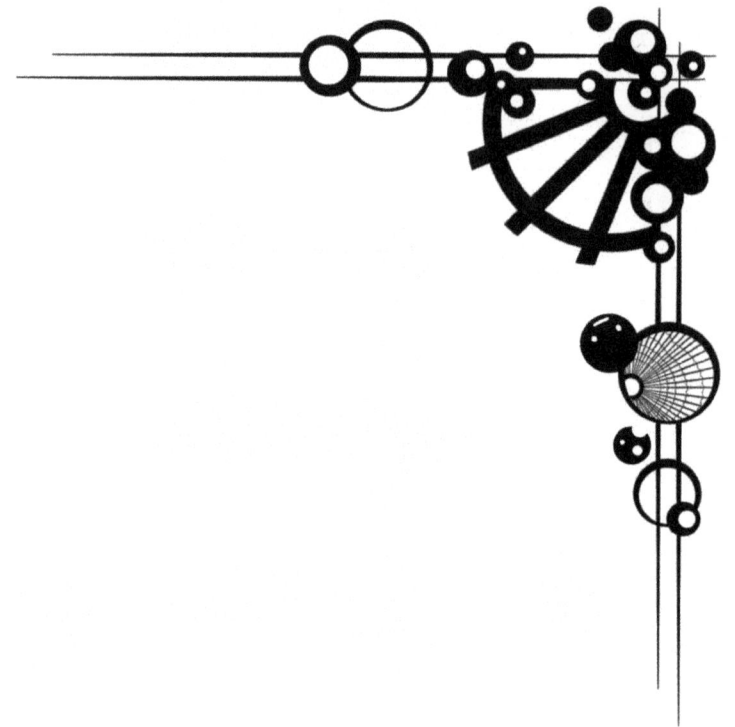

"Before you set the table, count the forks and spoons, glasses, napkins, plates...the guests will arrive soon!"

I triple check my list. It seems to all be there.
Having everything guarantees that all is fair.

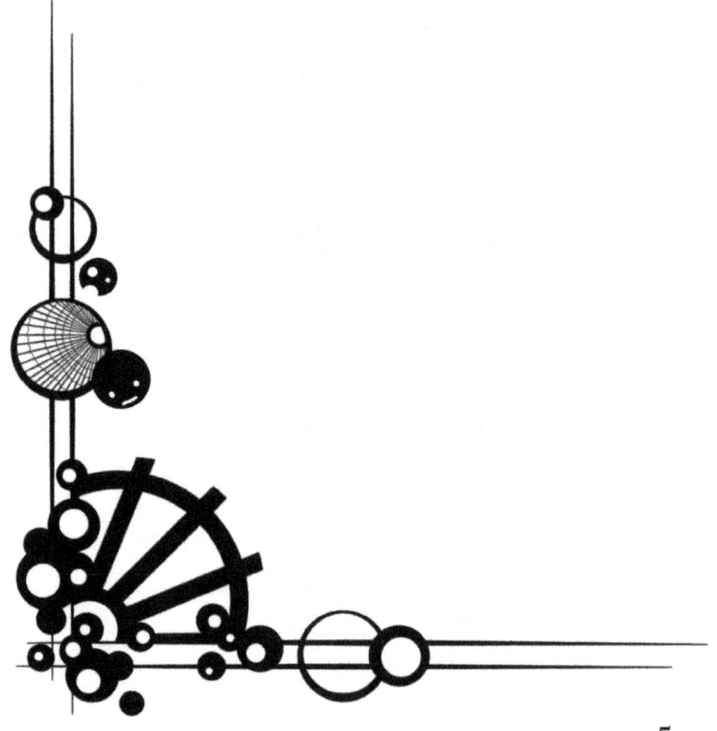

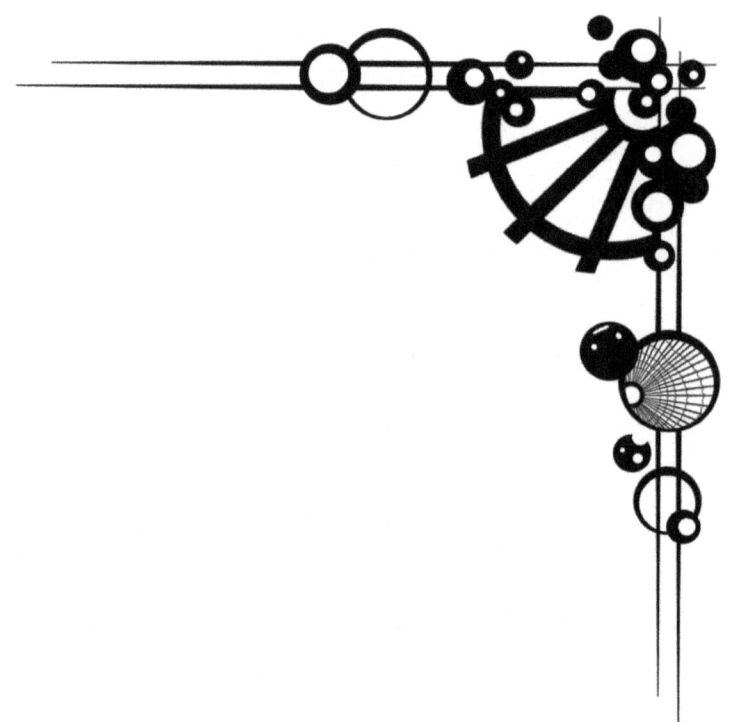

I go and wash my hands
to keep them nice and clean.

Nothing can be dirty.
That would just be mean.

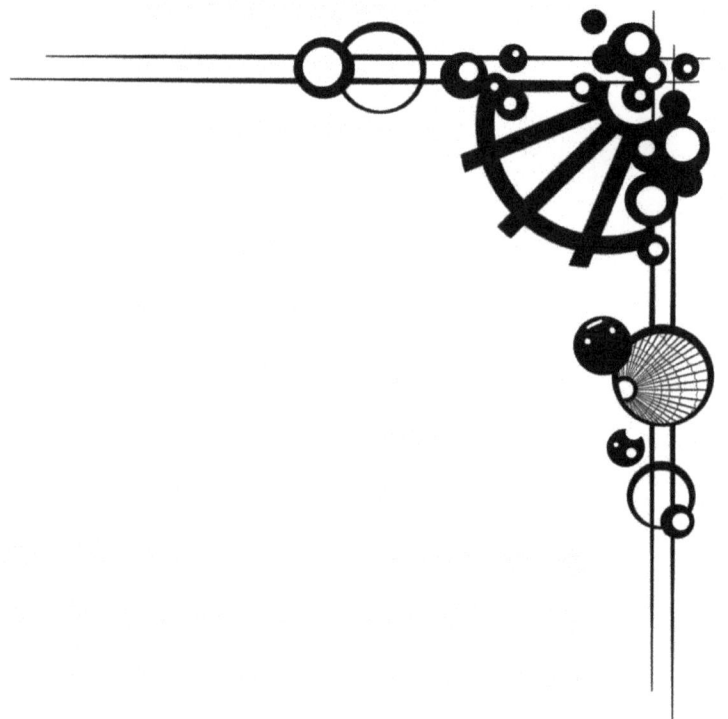

Time to set the table.
Look! The dishes gleam.

As mommy's little helper,
the setting makes me beam.

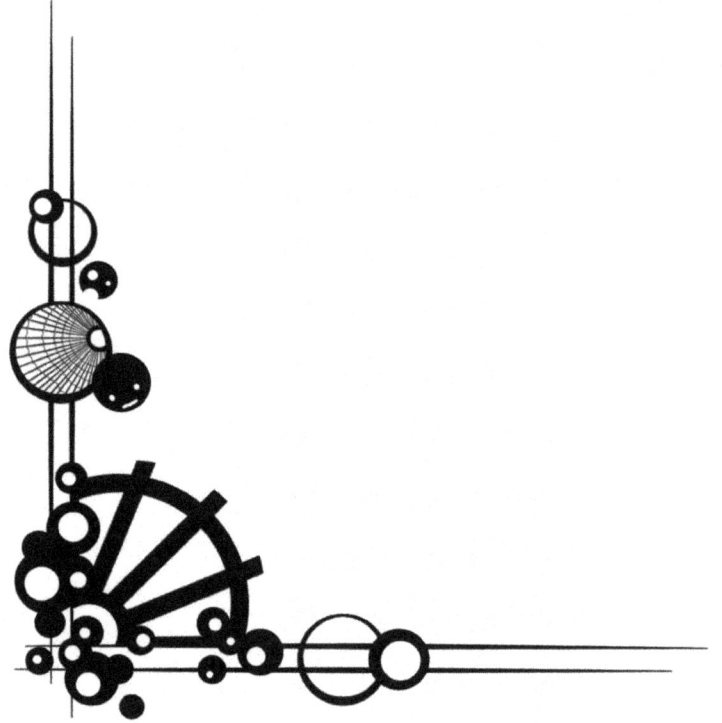

The guests begin to arrive, and everyone takes a seat.
We give our Lord thanks, and then begin to eat.

Our forks go on the left, spoons and knives go on the right.
My napkin's in my lap. My manners are out of sight!

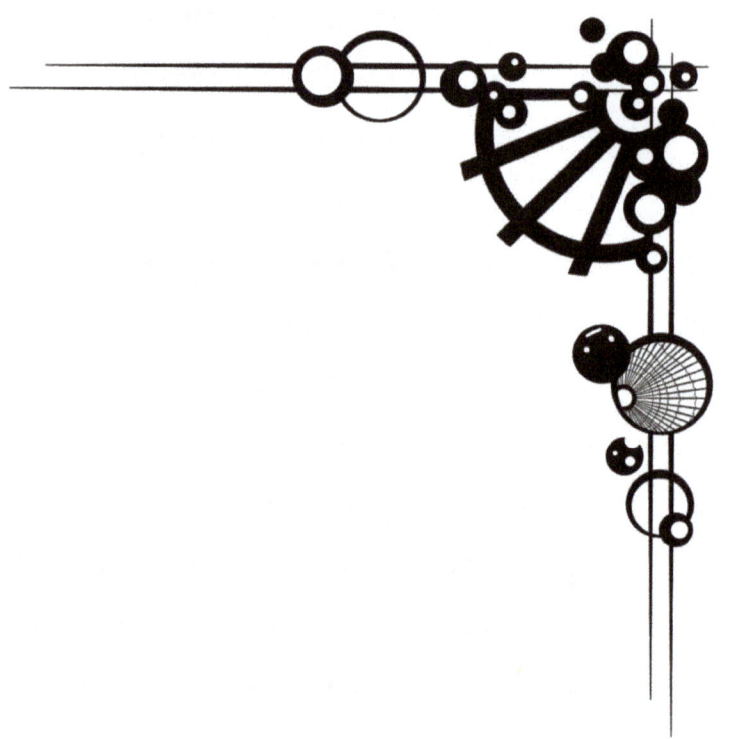

"When we sit and eat, you have to be neat."
"No playing around, and stay in your seat."

"Will you pass the peas and the bread, too?"
"Always say please, and say thank you!"

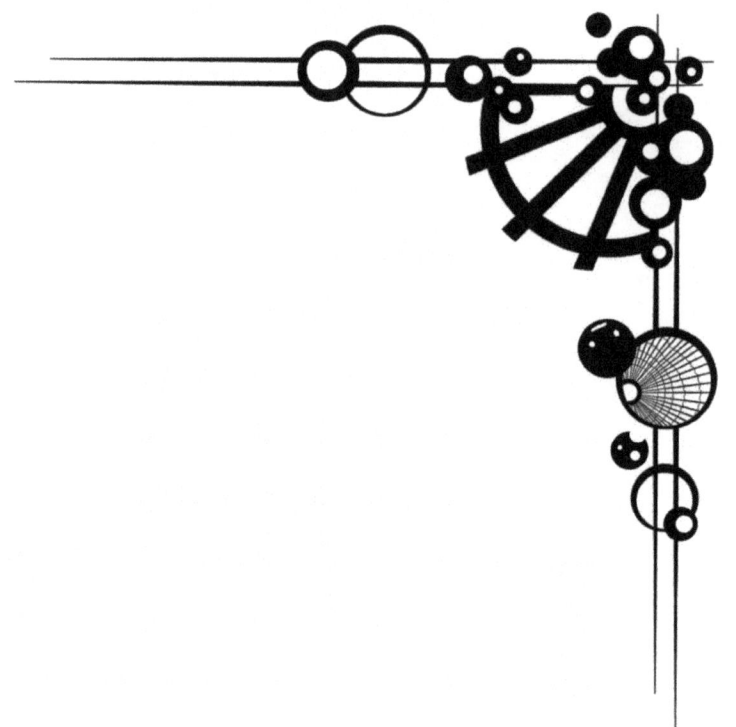

I've learned basic rules,
and that is so cool.

My friends are all here.
We'll take these rules to school!

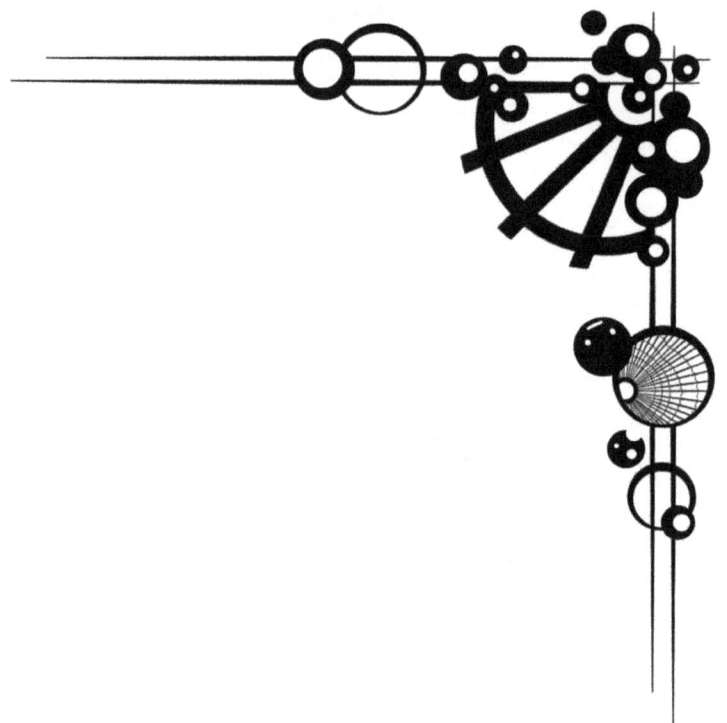

Our party time is over.
The guests begin to leave.

I wave one last goodbye.
It's been a good eve.

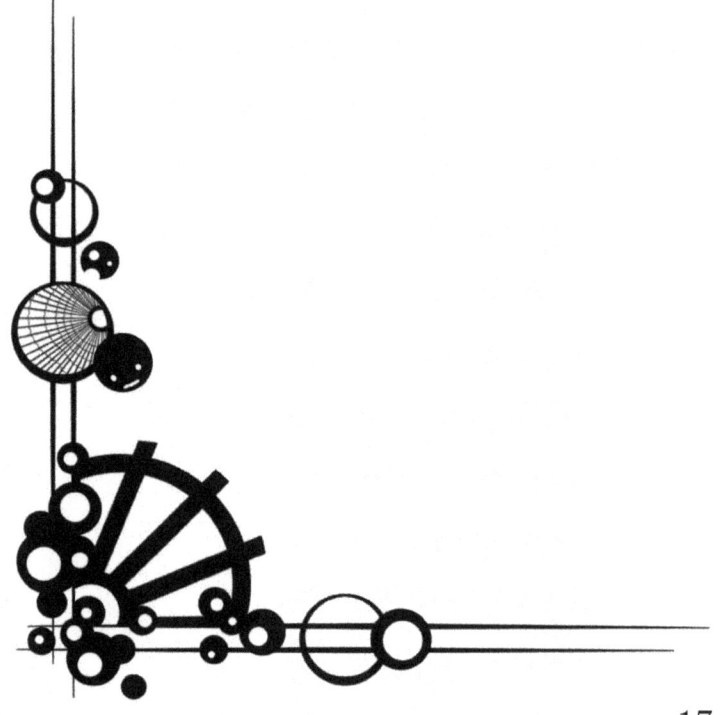

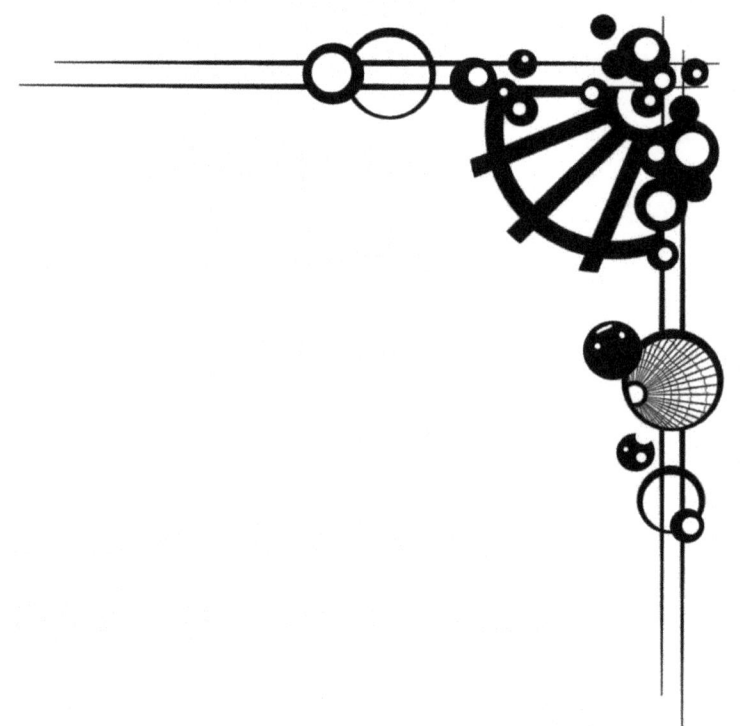

It's time to clean the dishes;
my least favorite part.

But I'm a good helper,
I know I must start.

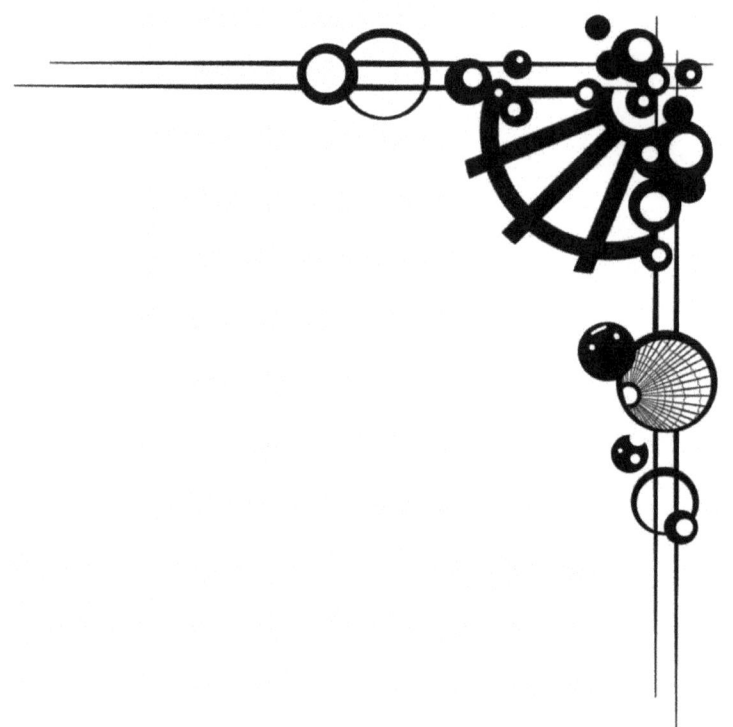

We finish the dishes quickly,
and now it's time to rest.

I'm so very thankful
and feel totally blessed.

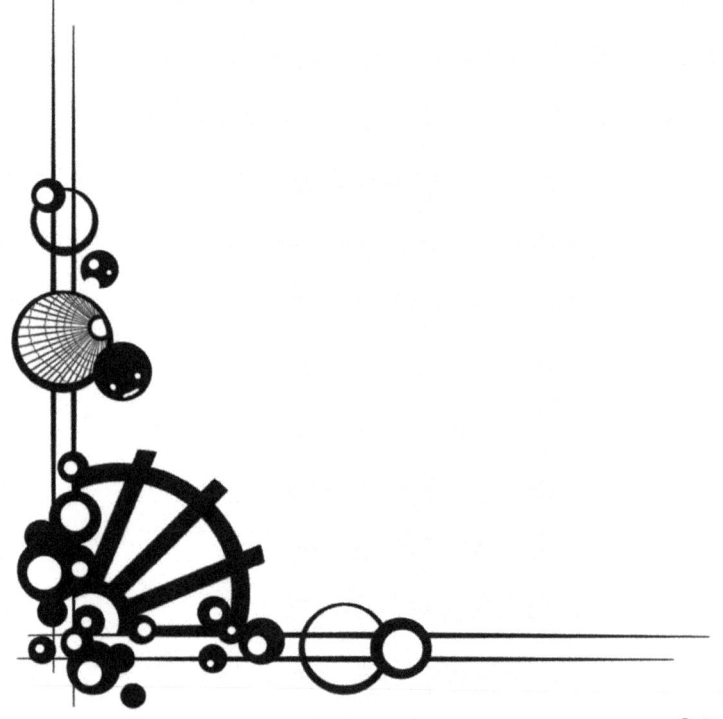

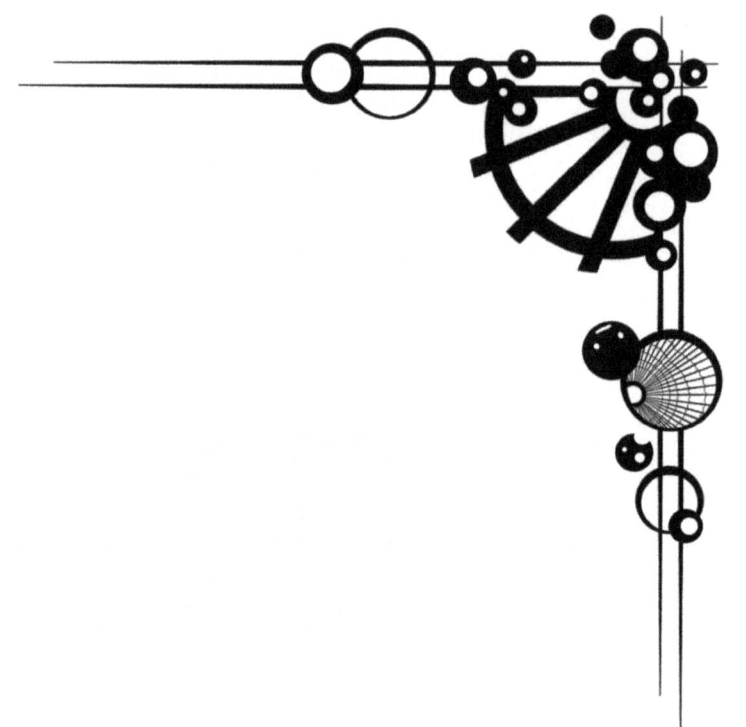

I hop right in bed and think about the day.
My first dinner party was a hit, I dare say.

Etiquette is cool and fun no less.
Etiquette's fantastic! It's simply the best!

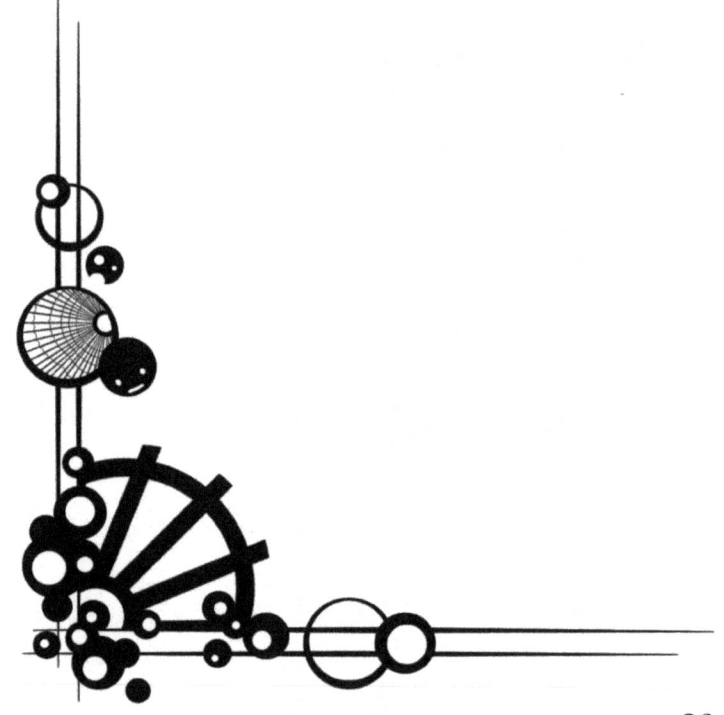

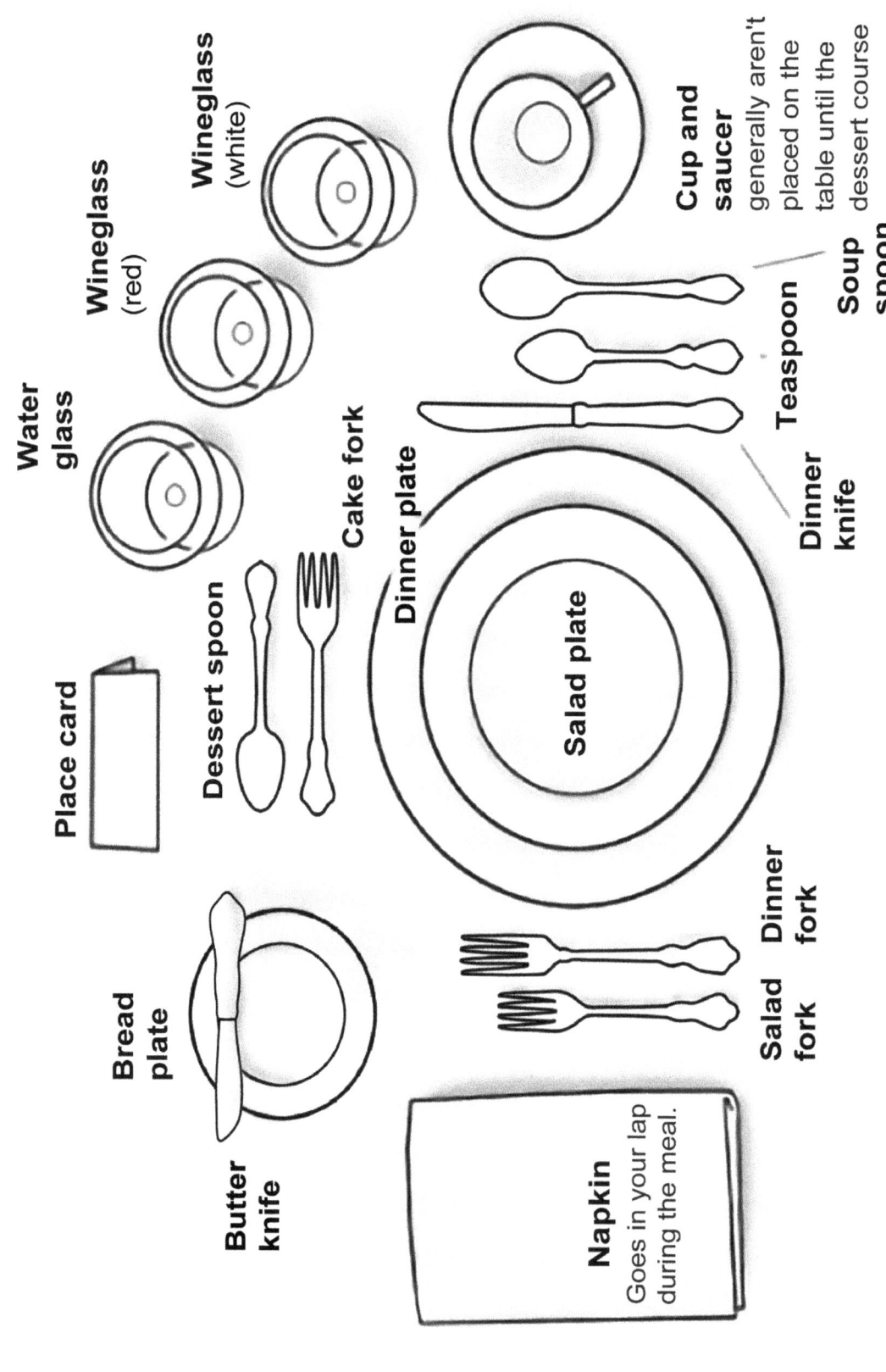

b & d

Left hand forms a "B".
B is for Bread. This is your Bread plate

Right hand forms a "D".
D is for Drink. This is your drinking glass.

Start from the outside then work in.

Make hand signs before you begin.

D is for drink, and B is for bread.

Now you have it in your head!

Enjoy the Music for "Etiquette is Fantastic"

https://youtu.be/xW4pxNHxj28

Song: "Etiquette is Fantastic"
Songwriter: Kenyae L. Reese, PhD
Producer: Christopher Blackmon

Vocalists:
Kenyae L. Reese, PhD
Gael Alcala
Valentina Alcala
Irie Burum
Braeden Carlton
Rosa Underwood
Donna Blackmon

www.ingramcontent.com/pod-product-compliance
Lightning Source LLC
LaVergne TN
LVHW070219080526
838202LV00067B/6862